W9-BIO-031

GOLF RULES

PLAIN & SIMPLE

GOLF RULES

PLAIN & SIMPLE

MARK RUSSELL
WITH JOHN ANDRISANI

Photos by Jeff Blanton

A HarperResource Book
from HarperPerennial

HarperCollins books may be purchased for educational, business, or sales promotional use. For information, please write to: Special Markets Department, HarperCollins Publishers, Inc., 10 East 53rd Street, New York, New York 10022.

FIRST EDITION

Text design by Stanley S. Drate / Folio Graphics Co. Inc.

Library of Congress Cataloging-in-Publication Data

Russell, Mark, 1951–
    Golf rules plain and simple / Mark Russell with John Andrisani : and photos by Jeff Blanton.—1st ed.
        p.   cm.
    ISBN 0–06–273668-X
    1. Golf Rules.   I. Andrisani, John.   II. Title.
GV971.R97   1999
796.352'02'022—dc21   99-22638
                                                                        CIP

99 00 01 02 03 HADD 10 9 8 7 6 5 4 3 2

Contents

Acknowledgments

First and foremost, we thank Damon P. Smith, of J.P. Morgan & Company, for hosting a dinner party at The Willet House, an historic restaurant in Portchester, New York. That's where we, along with John Bannon of Chapdelaine & Company, met and, together, conceived the idea to write this book, which makes learning the rules fun.

We both have great respect for the United States Golf Association and the Royal and Ancient Golf Club of St. Andrews, Scotland, and their book, *The Rules of Golf.* Having said that, we think the book you are about to read will educate you on the rules quickly and prepare you to appreciate the efforts behind the preparation of *The Rules of Golf.*

Special thanks are extended to Timothy W. Finchem, Commissioner of the PGA TOUR. We knew we had a winning book when we read the fine words he had to say about it in the foreword that follows.

We extend our gratitude to our agent Scott Waxman, of the Scott Waxman Agency in New York, and Robert Wilson, editor at HarperCollins Publishers, for believing in this book.

We thank all the folks at Orange Tree Golf Club in Orlando, Florida, namely the Wisne family, who own this great facility, and Nick Bianco, the club's general manager. We thank, too, photographer Jeff Blanton, along with models Kelly Fusco, Michelle Peters, and Jenks Wheelis.

We thank artist Shu Kuga, for the fine illustrations contained in this book.

We are also grateful to Wade Cagle, Jack Tuthill, Slate Tuttle, George Boutell, Tony Wallin, the members of the PGA TOUR Rules Committee, together with the knowledge passed on to us by the late Clyde Mangum and Marler S. Tuttle.

We also thank some other individuals who were not involved directly with *Golf Rules Plain & Simple* but were part of a great support team. This list includes Laura and Alexandra Russell, Richard G. Phillips, Joe "Mr. Big" Petrovich, and Steve Carmen.

MARK RUSSELL and JOHN ANDRISANI

Foreword

Playing by the rules of the game is an integral part of the competition on the PGA TOUR.

Golf may be unique in the fact that players throughout the world play by the same rules as written and defined by the United States Golf Association and the Royal and Ancient Golf Club of St. Andrews.

While the PGA TOUR, as is the case with any other tournament-organizing body, retains the right to make rules specific to its own competitions, we support the USGA and the R & A in their role as the rules arbiters of the game.

The rules officials on the PGA TOUR are there to assist our players on the PGA TOUR, and it is not unusual for a player to call a penalty on himself for any breach of the rules. It is one of the traditions of the game that sets golf apart from other sports.

It is unlikely that you have a rules expert to assist you in playing by the rules all the time, so we hope that this book—written by PGA TOUR Tournament Official Mark Russell and veteran golf writer John Andrisani—will help your understanding of the rules and how you can apply them in tournament situations or in casual play with your friends.

Mark has done an excellent job of utilizing real rules situations to identify the most common mistakes by golfers everywhere. Using this approach, Mark makes the rules easier to comprehend.

Understanding the rules of this great game allows a player to enjoy it to the fullest.

TIMOTHY W. FINCHEM
Commissioner, PGA TOUR

Preface

I would never call golfers cheaters. That's because I feel wholeheartedly that most recreational players realize that golf is a game of honor. Having said that, I'm surprised that there are not more arguments among players competing in friendly matches. The reason is, I have been a witness to weekend golfers violating the rules. Sadly, I have played with numerous amateur golfers who have absolutely no clue what to do when they hit the ball in a water hazard marked by red or yellow stakes, find the ball in casual water, hit the wrong ball, or discover the ball on a cart path. These are basic situations that come up often during a round of golf. Yet, if nine out of ten golfers were given a test on the correct rule procedures involved, they would fail.

I once lived on a golf course in Florida; the name of which I choose not to mention for fear it could cause embarrassment to that facility and its patrons. I say this because, day after day, while writing magazine articles or working on instructional books for publishers, I would be a witness to golf-rule misdemeanors. The most classic "crimes" involved lost ball or out of bounds violations. Player after player, who hit his or her ball out of bounds, would pick it up and toss it out sideways. When the typical player lost a ball, he or she would retrieve a new ball from the bag and do the same. In both instances, I would hear the player say, "I'll just drop one here and play three." When you hit a ball out of bounds or lose it, you must penalize yourself one stroke and then return to the spot where you last played a shot. I will not bore you with other firsthand accounts of players I saw breach the rules while looking out my office window. Suffice to say the list is a long one.

My experiences, when either paired with golfers on the course or watching them play from my window, caused me to shake my head in disbelief. At times like these, I wished that players had to pass a rules exam before they were allowed on the course, as is the case in many European countries. I'm bothered by this state of affairs involving the rules, simply because if you do not play by them you can't turn in a true score. Therefore, the handicaps of players can not possibly be honest, which makes playing in tournaments somewhat of a black comedy.

I became so frustrated by this situation that, a couple of years ago, I decided to survey golfers. I asked golfers I played with, or met in the 19th hole, if they had ever read *The Rules of Golf,* written and published by the United States Golf Association in Far Hills, New Jersey. Surprisingly, most players said that they "tried to." When I inquired further, the consensus was that they had trouble looking up a rule in the book's contents page. Moreover, once they found a rule, they couldn't clearly understand it. I had one player tell me, *"The Rules of Golf* is filled with so much legalese that, every time I need an on-the-spot ruling and turn to a page in search of an answer to a rules question, I feel I need to get F. Lee Bailey on the cellular."

Some time after, while reading "The Ruling Class" article in the GolfPlus section of *Sports Illustrated,* renowned golf writer John Garrity commented: "The rules book is a mildewed pamphlet crammed with legalese and hypotheticals."

I wouldn't go that far. Furthermore, I don't want you to get the impression that I believe the USGA did a poor job of presenting the rules in their official book. Golf is, after all, a very precise game that requires exactness when interpreting the rules, just as it does when hitting a shot. *The Rules of Golf* is a very comprehensive book that every golfer should read, over and over and over again, until it's understood. Equally as impressive is the *Decisions on The Rules of Golf,* put out by the USGA and the Royal and Ancient Golf Club of St. Andrews. All the same, for a long time, I have felt that something was needed to help golfers learn the rules more easily and more quickly.

My frustrations with "rules-confusion" the formal rules book prompted me to talk to Mark Russell, a rules official for the PGA TOUR. We talked at length about the problem of what to do about the majority of golfers not knowing how to deal with even the most elementary on-course rules situations. Things really got interesting when I told Mark about a past forum that George Peper, the editor-in-chief of *GOLF Magazine,* and I conducted with about a half dozen professionals on tour. These big-name pros, who at the time were on the editorial staff, admitted that they, themselves, were sometimes not sure of a rule.

Something else I told Mark presented him with proof that average players truly want to play by the rules, and not consciously cheat, which is the way it often appears. The "Within the Rules" page that ran every month in

GOLF Magazine was the most popular page, according to in-house surveys. As a matter of note, I'm told it still is. When I informed Mark about one more fact, he, like me, was convinced that golfers would be interested in buying a simply written rules book. A few years earlier, *GOLF Magazine* had offered a plastic bag-tag with The 10 Golden Rules printed on the back. Only about six of the most common rules situations were simply explained, yet thousands and thousands of bag-tags were sold.

Eventually, Mark and I got together at a dinner party in Portchester, New York, hosted by J.P. Morgan & Company. John Bannon, a best friend, low-handicap player, and partner at Chapdelaine & Company, a national bond-brokerage firm based in New York, was a guest at the party. He suggested Mark and I write a book simplifying the rules. We agreed right then and there to begin work on this project. We decided, too, that, in order to make the rules-message even simpler to understand, photographs and drawings—not contained in *The Rules of Golf*—would be included in our book.

What you now hold in your hands proves that we kept our promise to ourselves, and to our publisher, Harper-Collins, to produce a book that would help America's twenty-six million golfers interpret the rules. *Golf Rules Plain & Simple* is our best attempt at providing you with a guidebook for making an on-course ruling, quickly and accurately.

It's designed in such a way that it is easy to reference any rule. The next time you, your match play opponent, a fellow medal play competitor, or a member of your weekend foursome has a question about what to do, concerning any common rules situation, you will be able to answer it. I, with the help of my co-author, have stripped the rules down to the bare bones. This book not only covers the most basic rules, but everything from what to do when an opponent asks you for advice on club selection to what happens when a player waives the rules is also here. The book reviews perplexing rules situations that amateurs and pros are confronted with on the course, along with the most common mistakes made and explanations of the correct procedures. Therefore, there is no excuse for not knowing what rule applies and what penalty relates to the relevant infraction.

Golf Rules Plain & Simple makes the process of learning the rules so easy that you can learn them in one sitting—and have fun doing so. You may not be able to memorize all of the thirty-seven rules contained in this book, but when you are through reading them I believe you will be better able to understand *The Rules of Golf*, and so educated that you could pass a test on the subject. For argument's sake, say you couldn't. Don't worry. The book is purposely designed to be simple, durable, and flexible, so you can just toss it in your golf bag and pull it out when you need it. If you run into a problem on the course, just turn to the contents and then refer to the appropriate rule. One quick read of the section on the common mistake will prevent you from doing the wrong thing—and being either penalized or disqualified. Moreover, reading the explanation of the correct procedure will tell you what to do. It's as simple as referring to a map to help you find out how to get to your destination as quickly as possible. In fact, that's the other bonus of keeping this book close at hand. It will allow you to play by the rules with no fear of delaying play. *Golf Rules Plain & Simple* will allow you and your friends to solve a rules problem yourself, because everything you need is truly at your fingertips.

Good luck and have fun playing by the rules.

JOHN ANDRISANI
Orlando, Florida

Introduction

Looking back, much has changed dramatically in the golf world, particularly over the last two decades—except one thing: Average golfers didn't know the rules then, and they don't know them now.

Some of you high handicappers might think I'm referring to you alone. I'm not. When it comes to naiveté about the rules, golfers who play at all handicap levels—novices and veteran players alike—lack a *full* understanding of how to proceed correctly on the course.

There's no need to feel embarrassed about not being a rules expert. The rules, as laid down by the USGA and R & A, in *The Rules of Golf*, are extremely detailed and precise. That's because this booklet is designed to handle the numerous situations that can and do arise during a round of golf.

Golf Rules Plain & Simple, the book you are about to read, is not complex, yet it will teach you a lot about the rules. This book is short and simple, yet so informative that it will help you learn the correct procedures for dealing with such course situations as those that follow: lateral water, an embedded ball, touching the line of a putt with a club, removing a loose impediment from a bunker, and waiting too long for a putt to drop into the hole. After reading *Golf Rules Plain & Simple*, you will know how to handle these situations, and many others, quickly and correctly. The knowledge you gain will help you solve many rules problems during your Saturday and Sunday game.

Golf is a game played over approximately 150 acres of land and under all types of conditions. The rules are the same for all players, whether they are amateurs competing in a weekend Nassau game, or professionals competing for millions in prize money. The trouble is, when people start playing golf they are concerned about their swing technique, not the rules that govern the game. It is not until they become proficient enough at golf to compete in club tournaments that they have to deal with the rules. Many golfers would like to play by the rules, but the majority of them do not even know the basics or how to apply them.

Golf Rules Plain & Simple was purposely designed to be golfer-friendly, in order that enthusiasts like yourself either learn the rules or be able to reference them easily.

In this book, I—and my coauthor John Andrisani—cite thirty-seven rules situations that all golfers deal with frequently, then explain each simply. We even list the exact place in *The Rules of Golf* where these situations can be found. By making this presentation, we hope to help golfers use the rules book and make them familiar with the most fun way to play the game of golf, which is by the rules.

Also included in *Golf Rules Plain & Simple* are "buzz-phrases" at the end of each rule, which will help those of you who just breeze through the book to pick up some important procedural pointers. Additionally, I have marked five Rule Situations—numbers 18, 21, 32, 34, and 36—with an asterisk. Learn only these and you'll be known as the rules expert of your weekend foursome.

If you think back over the years you've played golf, and recall the frustrations experienced when dealing with rule procedures on the course, you will want to read this book and recommend it to other players. If you do, golf will be a better game.

The contents and interpretations in this book are solely based on my own opinions on *The Rules of Golf.*

MARK RUSSELL
Orlando, Florida

GOLF RULES

PLAIN & SIMPLE

RULE SITUATION

Asking for Advice on Club Selection

SITUATION: Player C has just picked the tee peg out of the ground after hitting an iron shot to a par three hole. Player D is Player C's match play opponent.

COMMON MISTAKE: Player D, who is ready to play next, breaches Rule 8–1 of *The Rules of Golf* by asking Player C what club she hit.

You are not allowed to ask or give an opponent for advice on club selection. You are, however, allowed to seek advice on the rules or matters of public information, such as asking an opponent what is the yardage number on a sprinkler head he or she is standing next to.

The penalty for asking advice during a match play competition is loss of hole. Match play refers to a hole-by-hole format. The player with the lowest score wins the hole. The player who wins the most holes wins the match.

In a stroke play tournament, Player D would be penalized two strokes for the same infraction. Stroke play is a form of play that determines the winner by the fewest number of strokes taken for the round.

In either match play or stroke play, the golfer who has the lowest score on a particular hole has the honor of hitting first on the following hole.

You are not allowed to ask your opponent
what club she hit.

You can look at your opponent's bag, however, to see which club she chose.

CORRECT PROCEDURE: In the aforesaid situation, Player D is allowed to watch what club Player C selects from her bag. As a matter of further interest, you and your four-ball match partner, and your caddies, are permitted to consult with one another and seek advice on club selection.

BE CAREFUL WHOM YOU ASK FOR ADVICE.

2

Ball at Rest Moved After the Player Addresses It

SITUATION: When Player A sets the club down on the grass and takes his address in preparation for his second shot, his ball moves out of its original position. Technically, you have addressed the ball when you have taken your stance and also grounded the club. (In a hazard, you are considered to have addressed the ball when you take your stance. The reason being, the rules of golf do not permit you to ground the club in a hazard.)

COMMON MISTAKE: Player A re-addresses the ball and then hits his approach shot onto the green of a par four hole being played. Player A takes two putts and believes he scored four on the hole. Wrong! Player A is to incur a two-stroke penalty, which is the general penalty for breaching Rule 18. The same breach of Rule 18–2b would cause him to lose the hole to a match play opponent.

CORRECT PROCEDURE: Once you address the ball and it moves out of position, you should penalize yourself one stroke. A ball is considered to have moved if it left its original position and came to rest in any other place. If the ball moves, you should inform your opponent. Next, you must place the ball back in its original position to avoid being penalized a total of two strokes. If you don't know the ball's exact position it must be dropped.

The ball moved, falling into a divot hole, after the player addressed it. If this happens to you, don't just re-address it and play on, as the player is getting ready to do here.

Instead, since you know the exact spot, place the ball back in its original position, as the player is doing here.

WHEN ADDRESSING THE BALL, YOU ARE AT RISK.

3

Ball in Motion Strikes Player's Golf Cart

SITUATION: On a par five hole, Player C shanks a short pitch third shot, meaning that the neck or hosel of the club, rather than its sweet spot or central portion of the clubface, contacts the ball. The ball darts off to the right, practically at a ninety-degree angle, hits Player C's motorized golf cart, and then rebounds onto the green.

COMMON MISTAKE: Player C picks the ball up off the green before dropping it next to the spot where it contacted her cart. Next, she chips the ball close to the hole. Finally, she puts the ball into the cup, for what she believes is a score of five.

Player C violated Rule 19–2. When a ball in motion is deflected accidentally by a player's own equipment, the player loses the hole in match play and is penalized two strokes in stroke play. As a matter of note, Player C would also be penalized two strokes for picking up a ball in play and not replacing it.

CORRECT PROCEDURE: Player C should have played her fourth shot from the spot where the ball came to rest on the green, after penalizing herself two strokes. In match play, she should have lost the hole to her opponent.

HITTING YOUR OWN EQUIPMENT IS COSTLY.

If your ball hits your own equipment and then rebounds onto the green, don't pick the ball up (*top*). Instead, penalize yourself two strokes and play the ball as it lies (*bottom*).

4

Ball Not Fit for Play

SITUATION: Player A's tee shot hits a cart path. After finding his ball and marking the spot with a coin, he lifts the ball and notices it has been cut and severely scuffed.

COMMON MISTAKE: Player A puts down a new ball and plays a shot to the green. When arriving on the green, Player B, Player A's match play opponent, notices the new ball with a different number on it. Player B then informs Player A that he has just lost the hole for not complying with Rule 5–3, which concerns the question of justifiably putting a new ball in play. Player A, for playing a shot with the substituted ball and failing to make his intentions

If you think your ball is sufficiently damaged to warrant removing it from play *(left)*, make sure you first consult with your match play opponent *(above)* or fellow stroke play competitor.

clear to his match play opponent, would be penalized one stroke. Had this been a stroke play event, Player A would also be penalized one stroke for the same breach.

CORRECT PROCEDURE: Before marking and lifting the ball to check for damage, and before switching balls, Player A should have announced his intention to Player B and given him the opportunity to examine the ball. If there is a question about whether the ball you are playing is sufficiently damaged to warrant removing it from play, speak first to your match play opponent or a fellow stroke play competitor. In actuality, you are entitled to take a ball out of play if it is cut or out of round.

KNOW WHEN YOUR BALL IS UNFIT FOR PLAY.

5

Bending or Breaking Branches

SITUATION: Player C, the match play opponent of Player D, discovers her ball under a tree in the rough. In preparing to play her next shot, Player C determines that an overhanging branch will prevent her from making a free backswing.

COMMON MISTAKE: Player C bends the branch back in such a way that she can now make a free backswing. She then plays her approach shot.

According to the rules, you are not permitted to bend or break anything growing or fixed if it improves the lie of the ball, your stance, or your area of intended swing. Consequently, Player C loses the hole to Player D because she bent the branch back to improve the area of her intended swing. In a stroke play event, Player C would incur a two-stroke penalty for violating Rule 13–2 as set down in *The Rules of Golf.*

CORRECT PROCEDURE: Deem the ball unplayable and take a penalty and drop, or play the shot in the best way possible in order to make solid contact. Player C should have played the ball in such a manner not to require her to bend the branch and breach the rules. For example, she could have choked down on the club and made a shorter or flatter swing. Alternatively, she could have swung back and hit the branch, free of penalty, and swung down contacting the ball as solidly as possible.

If the branches of a tree prevent you from swinging back freely *(left)*, don't bend the branches back *(above)*.

Instead, find a way to avoid them.

DON'T BEND OR BREAK
THE RULES.

6

Brushing Line of Putt With Hands

SITUATION: Player A notices a few tiny pebbles on the line between the ball and the hole.

COMMON MISTAKE: Player A firmly brushes the grass on the line of the putt, in order to sweep away the loose impediments. He brushes the green so hard that he presses down the blades of grass, which violates Rule 16–1. The penalty for such a violation is two strokes or loss of hole, depending on whether you are competing in a stroke play or match play competition.

CORRECT PROCEDURE: Since there were only a few pebbles on Player A's line, he should have picked them up one by one. In such circumstances, you can also brush them away with your hand or the club, not a towel or cap, provided you do not change the characteristics of the green or test the surface of the green.

BE CAREFUL HOW YOU BRUSH AWAY NATURAL OBJECTS ON THE GREEN.

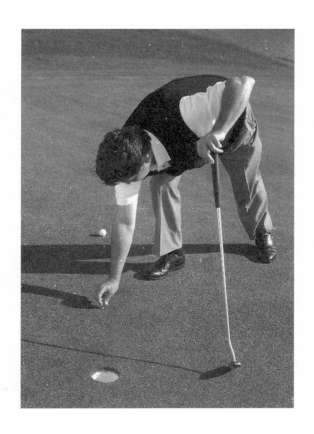

Don't brush away pebbles like this *(left)*. Rather, carefully pick them up off the green *(above)*.

7

Building a Stance in a Bunker

SITUATION: Player A's ball rests on a steep downhill lie next to the back of the bunker.

COMMON MISTAKE: In taking his stance, Player A finds it very difficult to feel balanced. Therefore, he digs his right foot deeper and deeper into the sand, in an attempt to essentially create a level lie. Still not comfortable, he lifts his right foot out of its deep print. Next, he kicks sand back into the hole left by his foot. Finally, he takes his address and plays the shot. Because he built a stance, he has just breached Rule 13–3. The penalty for building a stance is two strokes, or loss of hole in match play.

CORRECT PROCEDURE: In taking your stance in a bunker, you are allowed to wriggle and set your feet firmly in the sand. You cannot, however, build a stance.

NEVER BUILD A STANCE IN A BUNKER.

Building a stance in a bunker is a breach of the rules *(top)*. This is how you should take your stance *(bottom)*.

8

Caddy or Partner Stays Directly Behind the Player's Line While the Player Makes a Stroke on the Green

SITUATION: Player A, on the green, is being helped in lining up a putt by his playing partner, Player B, who is kneeling down about a yard behind the ball. Player B has his ball marked on the same line as Player A and wants to see how the ball breaks.

COMMON MISTAKE: Player B stays in the same position while Player A putts the ball. A partner or caddy is not allowed to do that, according to Rule 16–1f. Consequently, Player A and Player B lose the hole to their match play opponents. The reason: Player A's breach of the rule also assisted Player B. Had Player A been competing in a stroke play tournament, and his caddy made the same mistake that Player B did, he would have been penalized two strokes.

CORRECT PROCEDURE: When the ball is on the green, your caddy or your partner is allowed to help you figure out the break, determine the direction of the grain on the putting surface, align the putter's clubface squarely to the hole, or give you and other advice. For example,

It is not okay for your playing partner to stand ▶ directly behind you as you putt.

they can offer advice on the speed of the putt. Neither your caddy nor your playing partner, however, is allowed to remain directly behind your line to the hole while you employ your putting stroke. In fact, he or she must move before you trigger the stroke.

NOTE: Although standing behind the player during the execution of the stroke is prohibited on the putting green, a caddy or playing partner is entitled to remain behind the player while he or she is hitting the shot anywhere else on the course. Starting in the year 2000, however, a player's caddy or his or her partner will not be permitted to stand behind the player during the execution of the shot.

BE CAREFUL WHO IS STANDING BEHIND YOU.

◀ It is okay for your playing partner to give you advice on the line of the putt.

Carrying Too Many Clubs

SITUATION: Player A finishes the 7th hole and starts making his way, via a motorized cart, to the 8th tee. Player B points at Player A's bag and says, "You're carrying fifteen clubs—one too many." Player A's responds, "I know, but I have not used this extra putter, and I don't plan to. So, I am only really playing with fourteen clubs."

COMMON MISTAKE: Player A is wrong for carrying too many clubs and, as a result, breaches Rule 4–4. In determining the penalty in match play, Player A shall lose each hole where the breach occurred. Yet, even though he had finished playing seven holes, the maximum penalty is two holes. In stroke play, the penalty is two strokes for each hole at which the breach occurred. The limit is four strokes, however, which is the penalty Player A would incur in a stroke play event.

NOTE: Contrary to popular belief among amateur golfers, it does not make one bit of difference if you inform your opponent before a match that the extra club(s) in your bag will not be used. You will still be penalized.

CORRECT PROCEDURE: The best defense against being penalized is to show up on the first tee with no more than fourteen clubs. From the time you hit your first shot on the first hole, all your clubs are considered in play—whether you intend to use all of them or not.

COUNT YOUR CLUBS BEFORE YOU TEE OFF.

It will do you no good to plead your case to your opponent about not using an extra club in your bag.

Casual Water

SITUATION: Player A's ball comes to rest in an area of the fairway where a sprinkler head has leaked water.

COMMON MISTAKE: Player A exercises his right to deem the ball in "casual water," according to Rule 25–1. Once Player A makes that decision, however, he lifts the ball and then wrongly drops it in an area of dry fairway, four club lengths from the edge of the casual water. This rules violation will cost Player A the hole in match play or two strokes in stroke play according to Rule 25–1b.

CORRECT PROCEDURE: Player A should have gone to the nearest point of relief that avoids the casual water, then dropped the ball within one club-length from that point.

According to *The Rules of Golf,* casual water is any temporary accumulation of water on the course that is visible before or after the player takes his or her stance and is not in a water hazard. Dew does not meet the standard of casual water.

In determining whether you are standing in casual water, you are not permitted by the rules to "pump" your feet. Take your normal stance. After that, if you see any water, you are in "casual." You are therefore entitled to a free drop within one club-length from the nearest point of relief.

Here, the player's ball is in casual water, ▶
as defined by the rules.

If you are competing in a tournament, and there is doubt in your mind as to whether your ball lies in casual water, ask the advice of an official before proceeding.

WHEN IN CASUAL WATER, DON'T JUST CASUALLY DROP.

◀ He drops the ball, however, much too far away from where he should have.

Changing the Characteristics of Your Club During a Round of Golf

SITUATION: Player A, while competing in a stroke play tournament, walks off the ninth green frustrated, because he has just three-putted two holes in a row. He feels the problem could be his putter, rather than his stroke.

COMMON MISTAKE: He removes three small sheets of lead tape that the pro had put on the back of the putterhead before the round to help enhance his feel for the clubhead. He then putts out on hole number ten using that same putter. The scorer and a member of the tournament committee immediately inform Player A that he is disqualified for violating Rule 4–2, which forbids a player from purposely changing the characteristics of a club during a round of golf. Breaching this same rule while competing in a match play tournament would also result in disqualification.

CORRECT PROCEDURE: Once you start a round of golf, you are not permitted to alter the characteristics of your club, unless the club is damaged during the normal course of play. Damaging the club by intentionally slamming it into the ground does not count. If you do damage the club during the normal course of play, you are allowed to repair or replace the club, provided you do not unduly delay play. You also have the option of using that club in its damaged state, but only for the remainder of the round.

This player removes lead tape from his club during the round. Playing with this club will result in disqualification.

DON'T ALTER THE CHARACTERISTICS OF YOUR CLUB DURING PLAY.

Dropping the Ball the Wrong Way

SITUATION: Player A hit his ball in a ground-under-repair area and decides to take a drop.

COMMON MISTAKE: Player A drops the ball over his shoulder, hits his next shot onto the green, and then completes the hole by two-putting.

Because Player A dropped the ball incorrectly, according to the criteria set down in Rule 20–2, he is penalized one stroke. Had he been competing in a match play event, the same penalty would apply.

CORRECT PROCEDURE: When dropping the ball, stand erect with one arm fully extended at shoulder height. Next, let the ball fall gently out of your hand onto the ground. You are not permitted to manipulate the ball with your fingers to impart spin on it.

KNOW THE RIGHT WAY TO DROP A BALL.

The wrong way to drop. ▶

The right way to drop.

13

Fixing a Spike Mark on the Line of the Putt

SITUATION: Player A marks his ball on the green with a coin, picks it up, and cleans it, as allowed by the rules. He holds the ball in his hand until it is his turn to putt. While he's waiting his turn, he analyzes the line to the hole. In reading the break in the green, he notices a spike mark along the target line.

You are not allowed to tamp down or repair a spike mark, such as the one shown here.

COMMON MISTAKE: Player A tamps down the spike mark before putting his ball back down on the green and picking up the coin. Player B, his opponent in the finals of the country club's match play championship, informs Player A that he lost the hole for breaching Rule 16–1c. In a stroke play event, this same breach would result in a two-stroke penalty.

CORRECT PROCEDURE: You are allowed to repair ball marks or old hole plugs in your line, but not spike marks.

You are entitled, however, to fix a ball mark.

NEVER REPAIR SPIKE MARKS ALONG YOUR PUTTING LINE.

Grounding a Club in a Hazard

SITUATION: Player A, while playing a stroke play championship, discovers his ball in a sand bunker. (A sand bunker is a hazard. Grass-covered ground bordering a sand bunker, or within one, are not considered part of the hazard. A ball is in a bunker when any part of it touches a bunker.) Player A takes his address.

COMMON MISTAKE: In taking his address, Player A rests the bottom of the club on the ground, just as he would when hitting a shot off grass (when not a hazard). Rule 13–4 does not permit grounding the club in a sand bunker or water hazard. Hence, Player A must incur a two-stroke penalty. In a match play game, the penalty is loss of hole. Incidentally, the same penalties apply if you touch the sand with the clubhead during the backswing.

WORD TO THE WISE: Be careful in a hazard. It's an area of the course you must respect, or you run the risk of suffering serious consequences.

CORRECT PROCEDURE: When preparing to hit a recovery shot from a sand bunker (or a water hazard), make sure to keep the club elevated. The bottom of the club is not allowed to touch the sand, the surface of the water, or any area of ground inside the hazard.

In a bunker, you are not allowed to ground your club *(top)*.
Keep the clubhead raised above the sand *(bottom)*.

NOTE: While on the subject of the correct procedure, here are some of the other things you are permitted to do in a bunker as long as you don't test the condition of the hazard or improve the lie of your ball.

- You can touch the ground to prevent yourself from falling.
- You can touch the ground to remove a movable obstruction (i.e., aluminum can, piece of paper, etc.).
- You, or your caddy, can place extra clubs down in a bunker.
- In addressing the ball, or making a backswing, a player can touch any obstruction, plant or other growing thing with the club.

WARNING: NEVER GROUND YOUR CLUB IN A HAZARD.

Hitting the Wrong Ball

SITUATION: Player A and Player B, two opponents in a match play tournament, hit their tee shots about 230 yards. Both balls land in the fairway, thirty yards apart.

COMMON MISTAKE: Player A is sure the ball farthest from the hole is his because he sliced the shot. Therefore, he doesn't even bother to check the logo and number imprinted on the ball. Instead, he quickly hits the shot onto the green. Soon after, Player B looks down at the ball remaining in the fairway and realizes that it is not his. Player A hit Player B's ball. This violation of Rule 15 costs Player A the hole. It would cost him a two-stroke penalty if they were competing in a stroke play event. In order for Player A to record and return a valid score in stroke play, he would have to play the hole out with the correct ball, from its original position. If he failed to follow that procedure and tees off the next hole, he would be disqualified.

NOTE: There is no penalty for playing a wrong ball in a hazard. That's because you are not allowed to pick the ball up to identify it in a hazard.

CORRECT PROCEDURE: Get in the habit of using a pen to put a distinguishing personal mark on your ball, so you know it is yours. Also, don't hit a shot without first checking to see whether the ball you are addressing is yours.

MAKE SURE THE BALL YOU ARE ABOUT TO HIT IS YOUR BALL.

Before the round, it is a good idea to give your ball its own distinguishing marks.

16

Illegal Assistance (From Artificial Device)

SITUATION: Player B is competing on an unfamiliar tournament course. By modern standards, this course is unusual because it does not have yardage markers.

COMMON MISTAKE: Player B is not worried about the course lacking markers. The reason: he has a range-finder device in his bag that can measure yardage via a laser. Before addressing the ball to hit his approach, he pulls this gadget out of his bag, points it at the green, and reads the distance that appears on a small screen.

During a formal competition, according to Rule 14–3 you are not allowed to use an artificial device that may assist you in your play of a hole. Whether you are playing in a match play or stroke play competition, the penalty is disqualification.

CORRECT PROCEDURE: When there are no yardage markers on the course, either hire a caddy who knows the course, pace off the distance without delaying play, or simply eye up your shot as the great players from the past used to do.

NO ARTIFICIAL DEVICES ALLOWED.

Here, the player violates the rules by using ▶ an artificial device to help him gauge distance.

Indicating the Line

SITUATION: Player A's ball is near the base of a very steep bank behind the green. Player A is so close to the high slope that he is unable to see the flagstick, which is in the center of the green. He asks his caddy to remove the flagstick from the hole and lift it up high, so he can get a feel for the line of the shot.

COMMON MISTAKE: The caddy moves toward the fringe with the flagstick, closer to Player A. Next, the caddy raises the flagstick high into the air while Player A hits the shot. According to Rule 8–2, the caddy is not allowed to stand on the line of play and hold the flag in the air while the player hits a shot. This breach will cost you two strokes. The penalty in match play is loss of hole.

CORRECT PROCEDURE: The caddy is allowed, according to Rule 17–1, to stand by the hole and raise the flagstick, since this is considered tending the flag. The caddy also is permitted to move away from the hole and hold the flag in the air to help the player see the target line, provided he or she moves out of sight or away from the designated line before the player hits the shot.

KNOW WHAT YOUR CADDY CAN AND CANNOT DO.

The caddy is not allowed to move closer to the player and hold the flag in the air while the player hits the shot *(left)*. The caddy is allowed to stand by the hole and hold the flag high in the air while the player hits the shot *(right)*.

18*

Lateral Water Hazard

SITUATION: Player A hits a tee shot that flies 200 yards in the air and lands in the middle of a lateral water hazard. The ball last crossed the margin of the hazard 100 yards off the tee.

COMMON MISTAKE: Player A, who is competing in a stroke play event, ignores the point at which the ball last crossed the hazard line marked by red stakes. He drops the ball in light rough, adjacent to the hazard and in line with the spot where the ball splashed down 200 yards from the tee. He penalizes himself one shot and plays on.

First and foremost, Player A had no right to merely drop the ball out sideways, directly across from where the ball came to rest in the lateral water hazard. The penalty for breaching Rule 26, in stroke play, is normally two strokes. In this case, however, the tournament committee would probably consider Player A's actions a breach of the rules serious enough to warrant disqualification under Rule 20–7. In match play, Player A would lose the hole to his opponent.

CORRECT PROCEDURE: What follows are your five options available to you according to Rule 26.

1. Play the ball from inside the hazard and suffer no penalty.
2. Under the basic stroke and distance option, you can incur a one-stroke penalty and play another

---

*Learn this rule and you'll be known as the rules expert of your weekend foursome.

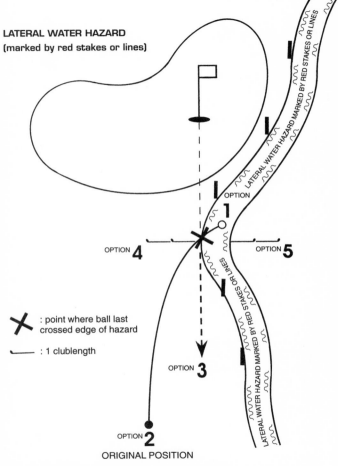

LATERAL WATER HAZARD
(marked by red stakes or lines)

LATERAL WATER HAZARD MARKED BY RED STAKES OR LINES

OPTION **1**

OPTION **4**

OPTION **5**

✗ : point where ball last crossed edge of hazard

‿ : 1 clublength

OPTION **3**

LATERAL WATER HAZARD MARKED BY RED STAKES OR LINES

OPTION **2**

ORIGINAL POSITION

This illustration will help you understand your options in a lateral water hazard.

49

shot from the spot where you played your original shot (which you hit into the hazard).

3. Under penalty of one stroke, you can keep the point where the ball last crossed the margin of the hazard between yourself and the hole, go back on that line as far as you would like, drop your ball, and play another shot from that point.

4. You can incur a one-stroke penalty, drop the ball outside the hazard two club lengths from the point where it last crossed the margin of the hazard, and play another shot from there. The ball can't come to rest nearer the hole than where it last crossed the margin of the hazard.

5. You can go to a point on the opposite side of the hazard that is equidistant from the point where the ball last crossed the margin of hazard, but is not nearer the hole. Once that point is determined, you can drop a ball outside the hazard, two club-lengths from this opposite point, under penalty of one stroke.

NOTE: If you drop the ball and it rolls back into the hazard, closer to the hole or out of bounds, you must re-drop according to Rule 20–2. On your second drop, if the ball again rolls back into the hazard, closer to the hole, or out of bounds, you are entitled to place the ball on the spot where it last struck the ground on your second drop. If, when placing the ball, you cannot get it to stay on the designated spot, you can place it as nearly as possible to that spot—but no nearer the hole.

KNOW YOUR FIVE OPTIONS IN A LATERAL WATER HAZARD.

Lifting an Embedded Ball

SITUATION: Player A's golf ball falls short of the green, embedding in the wet sandy bank of a regular water hazard marked by yellow stakes.

COMMON MISTAKE: Player A picks his ball out of the embedded lie. Then, he drops it next to the spot where it was embedded. He feels he's entitled to a drop because he knows that Rule 25–2 allows a ball embedded in its own pitch mark in a closely mowed area through the green to be lifted, cleaned, and dropped without penalty.

Player A has misinterpreted the language contained in the aforesaid rule. The phrase "through the green" refers to the entire area of the golf course, except the teeing area and the green of the hole being played, and any and all hazards on the course.

Because a ball in a hazard is not allowed to be removed from its "plug," Player A shall be penalized two strokes under Rule 18–2. He would lose the hole in match play.

CORRECT PROCEDURE: Player A can play the ball out of the embedded lie. Alternatively, he can exercise the option of acting under the yellow water hazard rule (Rule 26).

NOTE: If the ball is embedded through the green in its own pitch mark, a player may pick it up, clean it, and drop it without penalty, as near as possible to where it was embedded, but not nearer the hole.

When the ball is embedded in a hazard *(above)*, you are not to drop it *(right)* without incurring a one-stroke penalty.

WHEN THE BALL IS EMBEDDED, YOU DON'T ALWAYS GET RELIEF.

Lost Ball

SITUATION: Player C slices her tee shot into the woods. She and her playing partners look for five minutes, which according to *The Rules of Golf* is the time limit available to a player searching for a ball.

COMMON MISTAKE: Instead of returning to the teeing area according to rule 27–1, Player C simply tosses a ball into an area of fairway, located a few yards away from where she thinks her ball came to rest. Next, she plays her third shot from the fairway. If you make this same mistake, you will lose the hole in match play. In stroke play, you would probably be disqualified for seriously breaching Rule 20–7 and giving yourself a distinct advantage by tossing the ball out sideways. The stroke play penalty, for not acting according to the rules, is two strokes.

CORRECT PROCEDURE: The penalty for a lost ball is "stroke and distance," meaning that you must incur a one-stroke penalty and return to the place where you played your last shot.

When declaring a ball lost, don't simply toss the ball ▶ out sideways and penalize yourself a stroke, like this player does here.

Penalize yourself a stroke and then return to the teeing area. You are hitting your third shot.

DON'T GET LOST BY THE LOST BALL RULE.

Nearest Point of Relief

SITUATION: Player A's tee shot lands in a large area of ground under repair. His lie is okay, at best. He's not worried because he knows the rules entitle him to take relief from this area. He should be worried, though, because taking a drop at the nearest point of relief will cause him problems. Adjacent to the ground-under-repair area, there is a hedgerow so close to where he should drop that it will interfere with his swing.

COMMON MISTAKE: In weighing his options, Player A believes he's entitled to take relief from the hedgerow. In fact, it's not the hedgerow but the ground under repair from which he is taking relief. Player A doesn't know that, so he drops on the other side of the ground under repair and plays his second shot from there.

Player A is not entitled to drop the ball where he did. The area next to the hedgerow was where he was supposed to drop the ball, since that is the nearest point of relief from the ground under repair. This same breach of Rule 25–1b will cost you two strokes in stroke play or loss of hole in match play.

CORRECT PROCEDURE: Player A should have dropped the ball within one club length, not nearer the

---

*Learn this rule and you'll be known as the rules expert of your weekend foursome.

HOLE DIRECTION

In the first photo *(above)*, Mark Russell is pointing to the nearest point of relief, marked by a tee. In the second photo *(right)*, Mark Russell has not acted in accordance with the rules, because he dropped the ball in the "nicest" point of relief rather than the "nearest" point of relief.

hole, from the nearest point of relief that avoids the ground under repair. As luck would have it, however, this drop did not help him. Therefore, his best option would have been to play the ball out of the ground under repair.

DEFINITION: Nearest point of relief is the point where the ball would be in your stance, when you have satisfied four things:

1. The point must not be nearer the hole.
2. The point must be free of the area of your intended swing, in this case, the ground under repair.
3. The point must free the area of your stance from the ground under repair.
4. The point must free the lie of ball from the ground under repair.

Once you determine the nearest point of relief, you may drop the ball within one club length from that point, but not nearer the hole.

IT'S NOT THE NICEST POINT OF RELIEF, IT'S THE NEAREST POINT OF RELIEF.

Out of Bounds

SITUATION: Player B is competing in a stroke play event. On the fourth hole, a par five, he hooks his second shot toward the out-of-bounds markers. When he discovers the ball, it is out of bounds. He retrieves the ball and penalizes himself a shot.

COMMON MISTAKE: He drops the ball two club lengths from the nearest out-of-bounds stake. Next, he plays his fourth shot from that spot. Since Rule 27-1 applies here, Player B is in big trouble for not returning to the spot where he played his last shot and dropping a ball. The penalty is two strokes, although there is a good chance that this serious breach would cause Player B to be disqualified under Rule 20-7. The penalty is loss of hole in match play.

CORRECT PROCEDURE: If you hit a ball out of bounds, follow the same procedure that applies when you lose a ball outside a hazard—basic stroke and distance.

DEFINITION: The out-of-bounds line is defined by the inside edge of the white stakes at ground level. If only part of the ball is in bounds, the ball is in bounds. If white lines are used to mark the boundary line, the line itself is out of bounds.

WHEN HITTING A BALL OUT OF BOUNDS,
STAY WITHIN THE BOUNDS OF RULE 27-1.

When the ball lands out of bounds, don't penalize yourself a stroke and drop two club lengths from the boundary stakes *(left)*. Instead, take the same stroke penalty and return to the tee spot where you last played a shot *(above)*. Remember, the penalty is stroke and distance.

Playing a Provisional Ball

SITUATION: Player A thinks his 180-yard tee shot could be lost in the woods, so he plays a provisional ball—another shot, just in case the first one is lost. The provisional ball finishes 200 yards down the fairway. Then, he walks with his caddy to the area where he believes the first ball landed.

COMMON MISTAKE: After searching for the ball for about three minutes, Player A instructs his caddy to keep looking while he goes and plays a second shot with the provisional ball. The ball lands on the green. Player A then turns to his caddy and says, "Let's go," even though there is still a little over a minute left on the five-minute-limit clock to discover the first ball. Suddenly, Player A's caddy says, "I've got it."

Player A decides to play his original ball. He has now played a wrong ball. That's because, once he hit his approach shot with the provisional ball, which was beyond the point where the original ball lay, it became the ball in play.

The penalty for such a breach is loss of hole in match play. In stroke play, Player A would be penalized two strokes (under Rule 15–3), and he would have to play out the hole with the correct ball, which, in this case, is the provisional. If he failed to do that and then teed off on the next hole, he would be disqualified. The reason is, he would not have recorded a true score with a ball in play.

Once you play a shot with a provisional that is beyond the point where your original ball lay . . .

. . . you cannot go back and play the original ball that was found.

CORRECT PROCEDURE: Once you play a shot with a provisional that is beyond the point where your original ball is likely to be, you are committed by Rule 27–2B to play the entire hole out with that provisional ball. In the situation above, once Player A hit his approach shot with the provisional, the provisional ball then became the ball in play.

When you choose to play a provisional ball, you must tell your fellow competitor or match play opponent your intention. If you don't, the provisional ball automatically becomes the ball in play. Furthermore, you can only play a provisional ball for a ball lost outside a water hazard or out of bounds. If you play a provisional ball for a ball that you think is lost in a water hazard, it automatically becomes the ball in play.

PLAY THE HOLE OUT
WITH THE RIGHT BALL.

Playing Outside Teeing Ground

SITUATION: While competing in a stroke play competition, Player A hits a tee shot ten feet from the cup on a par three hole.

COMMON MISTAKE: Even though Player A hit a very good shot, he made the error of teeing up the ball more than two club lengths behind the tee markers. The penalty for such a breach is two strokes, plus Player A must correct his error by hitting another shot from the teeing area. In a match play event there is no penalty, but Player A's opponent has the right to ask him to re-tee the ball and play the shot again within the boundaries of the teeing area as defined by the rules. The same procedures would apply if Player A hit a shot from in front of the tee markers. He still would have played outside the teeing ground.

CORRECT PROCEDURE: When teeing off on a par three, par four, or par five hole, the player must tee off within a rectangular area two club lengths in depth from the tee markers. The front and sides of the imaginary rectangle are defined by the limits of the two markers. The ball is considered outside the teeing area when it lies fully outside the rectangle. Rule 11 covers the teeing ground.

KNOW WHERE THE TEEING GROUND STARTS AND STOPS.

Here *(top)*, the player hits outside the teeing ground.
Here *(bottom)*, the player prepares to hit the shot well
inside the boundaries of the teeing area.

Practicing During Play of a Hole

SITUATION: Player A is competing in a stroke play tournament, meaning that the winner will be the player with the lowest total score. He arrives at the course too late to practice, so he races to the first tee and drives the ball down the fairway.

COMMON MISTAKE: While his fellow competitors are teeing off, Player A runs over to the nearby practice putting green and hits a few putts. According to Rule 7–2, you are prohibited from practicing "during" the play of the hole. The penalty for such a breach is two strokes or loss of hole in match play.

CORRECT PROCEDURE: If you want to practice putting or chipping between the play of two holes, you must do that only on the green you last played, on a practice putting green, or on the next tee. Again, you cannot practice *during* the play of a hole.

THERE'S A RIGHT TIME AND A PLACE TO PRACTICE PUTTING AND CHIPPING.

This player is wrong to practice putting *during* the play of a hole.

Putted Ball Strikes Flagstick

SITUATION: Player A asks his caddy to attend the flagstick while he hits a putt from fifty feet. Tending the flag simply means holding the flag until the ball is struck and then pulling it. Players normally ask for the flag to be tended when they are far enough away from the hole that they are unable to see it clearly.

Player B, Player A's match play opponent, stands nearby waiting his turn to putt.

COMMON MISTAKE: The caddy does not pull the flagstick out before the ball arrives at the hole. In fact, the ball strikes the flagstick and rebounds off it, finishing five feet from the hole. Although Player A was not at fault, he still loses the hole for breaching Rule 17–3. In stroke play, you must play the ball wherever it lies after hitting the flagstick and penalize yourself two strokes.

CORRECT PROCEDURE: Whoever tends the flagstick while a player is putting, whether it is your caddy, partner, or fellow player in a weekend game, should know to remove it before the ball hits it. Get in the habit of removing the flagstick the split-second the ball is struck and starts rolling toward the hole.

KNOW THE RIGHT WAY TO TEND THE FLAGSTICK.

To avoid a problem on the green, and being penalized, ask your caddy or playing partner to pull the flagstick soon after the ball is struck.

*Removing a Loose
Impediment From
a Sand Bunker*

SITUATION: Player A's ball lands in a fairway bunker. He discovers that a small pinecone sits directly behind the ball.

COMMON MISTAKE: Player A believes that he is allowed to remove the pine cone. Player A's thinking is wrong. You are not allowed to remove a loose impediment from a bunker or water hazard. For your information, a loose impediment is referred to as a natural object—i.e., this pine cone, leaves, twigs, stones, insects, and mounds made by insects. Loose impediments do not adhere to a ball. Loose soil and sand are loose impediments on the putting green, but not elsewhere on the course.

Player A's breach of Rule 23–1 will cost him two strokes or loss of hole in match play.

CORRECT PROCEDURE: Play the ball as it lies, the idea being to dig the club more deeply into the sand behind the pinecone and try to blast the ball out. When applying the unplayable lie rule in this situation, there are three other options available to you, under penalty of one stroke:

You are not allowed to remove a pinecone—or any loose
impediment—from a bunker.

1. Drop the ball in the sand within two club lengths of the spot where the ball lay, but not nearer the hole.
2. Replay the shot from the point at which you hit the previous shot.
3. Go back as far as you like in the sand bunker and play a shot from that point, provided you keep the spot where the ball originally lay between yourself and the hole.

THERE ARE TIMES WHEN YOU ARE NOT PERMITTED TO REMOVE A LOOSE IMPEDIMENT.

Removing an Out-of-Bounds Stake

SITUATION: Player A's ball lands in bounds. Once Player A takes his stance, however, he determines that one of the white "o.b." stakes is in his way.

COMMON MISTAKE: Player A removes the stake, breaching Rule 13–2, and then plays the shot. This action is not permitted by *The Rules of Golf*. The penalty for such a breach is loss of hole in match play or two strokes in stroke play.

CORRECT PROCEDURE: Play the shot as best as possible while leaving the out-of-bounds stake in the ground (i.e., left-handed), or opt to take an unplayable lie and proceed accordingly.

Out of bounds is considered property off the golf course. When not marked by white stakes, out of bounds is usually defined by property line fences, walls, or roads. The out-of-bounds line is defined by the inside edge (on the golf course side) of the stakes at ground level. If any part of the ball is in bounds, the ball is in bounds. Understand, too, that you may stand out of bounds to play a ball that's in bounds.

AT NO TIME ARE YOU ALLOWED TO REMOVE AN OUT-OF-BOUNDS STAKE.

When blocked by an out-of-bounds stake, it's a breach of the rules to move it *(left)*. Instead, find a way to hit the shot, such as playing it left-handed *(above)*, or declare the ball unplayable.

RULE SITUATION

*Searching Too Long for a
Lost Ball*

SITUATION: Player A, while competing in match play, hits a slice off the tee that flies toward a trouble area located well right of the fairway. Player A and his caddy walk toward the spot where they think the ball is located. They search for the ball and find it after five-and-a-half minutes.

COMMON MISTAKE: Player A plays the shot and completes the hole. This mistake causes Player A to lose the hole.

CORRECT PROCEDURE: Player A should have been aware of the five-minute rule and timed himself. Once he saw or discovered that he passed the limit, he should have penalized himself one stroke, returned to the tee, and hit his third shot, according to Rule 27–1.

Note: Had this been a stroke play tournament, Player A would have been penalized two strokes for playing a wrong ball (Rule 15–3). The reason is, after searching for your ball for five minutes, it is to be declared lost, whether you find it or not.

Player A should return to the tee to play his third shot. If he teed off on the next hole without first doing that, he would be disqualified.

***WATCH THE FIVE-MINUTE CLOCK WHEN
SEARCHING FOR A BALL.***

When looking for a lost ball, remember that
you are always working against the five-minute clock.

30

Signing an Incorrect Scorecard

SITUATION: During a stroke play tournament, Player A scores birdie on hole number sixteen. Player B, who is keeping Player A's official score, pencils in a par three for that same hole.

COMMON MISTAKE: After the round, Player A quickly checks the scorecard made out by Player B signs it, then returns it to the tournament committee. Since the score recorded was higher than actually taken, and Player A attested the card, the score as returned shall stand in accordance with 6–6d. In the 1968 Masters championship, Roberto DeVicenzo, the great player from Argentina, signed a wrong scorecard. His fellow competitor and scorekeeper, Tommy Aaron, wrote down a four for DeVicenzo's score on hole seventeen, when he should have written down a three. Unfortunately, DeVicenzo attested the official card, so the score of four stood, making his total 66 instead of 65. Worse still, that mistake cost DeVicenzo the championship. American Bob Goalby was declared the winner.

As a matter of note, if Player A would have signed a card that showed a score lower than his actual score, he would have been disqualified in accordance with Rule 6–6d.

CORRECT PROCEDURE: You are responsible to yourself, and to your fellow players, for turning in an accurate score on each hole. So, before signing a scorecard and returning it to the committee, check every hole—twice!

Review your score before handing a scorecard over to the tournament committee.

**BEFORE SIGNING A SCORECARD,
MAKE SURE THERE'S A CORRECT SCORE
IN EVERY BOX.**

Touching the Line of a Putt

SITUATION: Player B, who is Player A's partner in a four-ball match, is analyzing the break in the green. Player A's ball is on the green.

COMMON MISTAKE: Player B touches the line of the putt with the head of his putter to indicate to his partner the spot where the ball will break dramatically. This is a breach of Rule 8–2b, which forbids touching the line from the ball to the hole. The penalty in match play is loss of hole. If you, or your caddy, were to touch the line during stroke play, you would be penalized two strokes.

You also are not allowed to lay a piece of grass, or any other object, down on the green to indicate the line of the putt.

CORRECT PROCEDURE: You are allowed to have your partner or caddy indicate the break in a green, say, by pointing at a spot on the target line. Your partner or caddy can also point the putterhead at the specific spot where the ball will start to break, as long as the club stays elevated above the surface of the green.

DON'T TOUCH.

When your ball is on the green, your playing partner is not allowed to touch the line with the putter *(right)*. He is permitted to point to a spot where he thinks the ball will break *(page 86)*.

Unplayable Lie

SITUATION: Player A discovers his tee ball in an area of trees, at the corner of a dogleg right hole—a hole that winds to the right. He knows that the ball is unplayable. Yet, taking the option to drop the ball within two club lengths of the spot where it lies and no nearer the hole, under penalty of one stroke, will not help him. That's because, after dropping the ball, it would still be so close to the trees that he would not be able to send it flying up quickly enough to avoid them. He also doesn't want to incur a one-stroke penalty, walk back to the tee, 210 yards away, and hit his third shot. He chooses the third available option, according to Rule 28 of *The Rules of Golf:* to walk back as far as he wants, keeping the point where the original ball lay between the hole and where he drops the ball.

COMMON MISTAKE: Player A penalizes himself one stroke and goes back fifty yards, believing he is keeping the point where the ball lay unplayable between himself and the hole. He considers his line of flight. The only trouble is, he walks back on such a sharp angle that, once he stops and drops the ball, he now can see the green so clearly that he can practically play a straight shot toward the green or, at least, a slight draw. In short, Player A has given himself an unfair advantage and, in doing this, has

---

*Learn this rule and you'll be known as the rules expert of your weekend foursome.

If your ball is unplayable *(above)* and you choose the
option to drop back, keep the point where the ball
originally lay between the hole and where you drop. Don't
do what this player did; don't determine a "line of flight"
and drop where you have a clear shot to the green
(right).

violated Rule 28-c, which governs how you should proceed when taking the option to drop a ball behind the point where the ball lay.

In match play, such a violation would result in a loss of the hole. In stroke play, Player A would be penalized two strokes for playing from the wrong place and one stroke for declaring the ball unplayable. This breach could cause Player A to be disqualified, according to Rule 20–7 that addresses playing the ball from the wrong place.

CORRECT PROCEDURE: If you choose option c of Rule 28, be sure to keep the point where the ball originally lay between the hole and the point where you drop. Line of flight is never mentioned in *The Rules of Golf.* It remains a myth of the game. It means nothing and is thus totally irrelevant when taking relief from an unplayable lie or any other rules situation.

LINE OF FLIGHT MEANS NOTHING.

33

Waiting Too Long for the Ball to Drop Into the Hole

SITUATION: Player C putts the ball toward the hole from fifteen feet away. The ball stops on the lip or edge of the cup and looks as if it may drop into it.

COMMON MISTAKE: Player C pauses for around five seconds before walking toward the hole. Then, she circles the hole for another ten seconds, waiting for the ball to fall into the hole. By now, she has unknowingly violated Rule 16–2. She then stands over the ball for another five seconds, hoping it will fall into the hole. It does. Player C is told by a member of the tournament committee that she waited too long for the ball to drop, so she is penalized one stroke.

CORRECT PROCEDURE: In such circumstances, do not linger where you last stroked the putt or by the hole. You have a reasonable amount of time to reach the hole. Once there, you can wait ten seconds for the ball to drop in. If it doesn't drop in that time frame, you must putt the ball into the hole.

WHEN THE BALL HANGS ON THE LIP, PAY ATTENTION TO THE TEN-SECOND COUNTDOWN.

Once you reach the hole, don't linger too long, waiting for the ball to drop *(above)*. You only have ten seconds for the ball to fall into the hole. Further, after the aforesaid time period, the ball is deemed to be at rest, and you must tap it into the hole *(right)*—even if it is moving.

34

What to Do When You Hit the Ball Into a Water Hazard Marked by Yellow Stakes

SITUATION: Player A hits the ball over a pond fronting the green. The ball lands on the bank, inside yellow stakes marking the hazard, and rolls back down into the shallow water.

COMMON MISTAKE: Player A believes that, since his ball carried the water and hit land, he is entitled to incur a one-shot penalty and drop outside the water hazard, near where the ball lay. Therefore, he lifts his ball from the water, climbs back up the bank, and drops the ball on land close to the green, then plays his next shot.

In match play, Player A would lose the hole to Player B, his match play opponent for breaching Rule 20–7a. In stroke play, Player A would be disqualified for a serious breach of Rule 20–7b, because he failed to negotiate the water hazard and did not correct his mistake.

CORRECT PROCEDURE: First and foremost, understand that the area of land inside the yellow stakes is part of the hazard. Player A may as well have hit the ball in the

---

*Learn this rule and you'll be known as the rules expert of your weekend foursome.

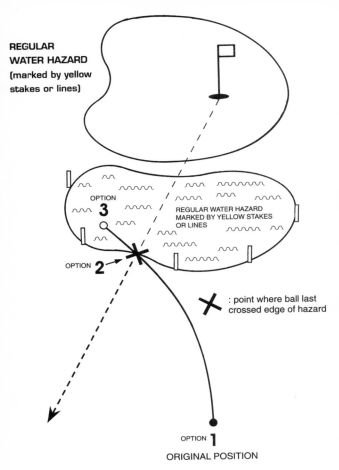

REGULAR
WATER HAZARD
(marked by yellow
stakes or lines)

OPTION
3

REGULAR WATER HAZARD
MARKED BY YELLOW STAKES
OR LINES

OPTION 2

✕ : point where ball last
crossed edge of hazard

OPTION 1
ORIGINAL POSITION

This illustration will help you understand your options
regarding a water hazard marked by yellow stakes.

water, because the options available to him according to *The Rules of Golf* are the same.

When you hit a shot into a yellow water hazard, your options under Rule 26–1 are as follows:

1. Go back and play a shot from the original spot from which you last hit the ball, and add one stroke to your score.
2. Keep the point where the ball last crossed the margin of the hazard between you and the hole, and go back as far as you like on that line. Drop the ball and, again, add one stroke to your score before playing another shot.
3. Play the ball from out of the hazard, under no penalty.

KNOW YOUR YELLOW-HAZARD OPTIONS.

35

When It's Wrong to Clean the Golf Ball

SITUATION: Player A's approach shot lands on a bank guarding the front of the green. When he arrives at the spot where his ball lies, he notices so much mud on it that he is not sure it is his.

COMMON MISTAKE: Player A marks the ball, lifts it to identify it, cleans off all the mud, then replaces it. According to Rule 21 of *The Rules of Golf,* in this situation Player A is permitted to clean only enough mud off the ball to identify it. The penalty for this breach is one stroke in both stroke and match play.

CORRECT PROCEDURE: Unless playing under the special circumstances of the lift-clean-and-place rule, as determined by the club's pro or the tournament committee, you are only allowed to clean the ball on the putting green or when taking relief from such things as casual water, ground under repair, embedded ball, or a movable or immovable obstruction.

YOU ARE NOT ALWAYS ENTITLED TO PLAY WITH A CLEAN BALL.

This player breached the rules by lifting the ball and cleaning it after it landed in a muddy area through the green. Normally, you are only allowed to clean the ball on the putting green or when taking relief from such things as embedded ball, casual water, ground under repair, or an obstruction.

36

When Taking Relief From an Immovable Obstruction— "Cart Path"

SITUATION: Player C finds her ball on a cart path, which she knows is considered an immovable obstruction. She also knows that, in this course situation, a free drop is allowed by the rules. You do not get relief from an immovable obstruction in a water hazard of any kind.

COMMON MISTAKE: Player C correctly considers the area of nearest point of relief before dropping the ball within one club-length from that point and no nearer to the hole. After the drop, the lie is such that she has to keep one foot on the cart path to play the shot. She decides to play the shot anyway, because the lie is so good. The ball lies on one of the few areas of grass in a very sandy area.

Player C is not allowed to keep one foot on the path after her drop, according to Rule 24–2. This breach costs her the hole in match play or a two-stroke penalty in stroke play.

---

*Learn this rule and you'll be known as the rules expert of your weekend foursome.

If you find your ball on a cart path, such as the type shown here *(above)*, you are entitled to a free drop. When dropping, however, make sure you take complete relief from the cart path *(right)* so that you can take your stance on the grass.

The mistake the player shown here made was not dropping far enough away from the cart path to give herself "complete" relief. Notice that her right foot is still on the cart path.

CORRECT PROCEDURE: When taking relief from an immovable obstruction (anything artificial) through the green, you must take complete relief. This procedure also applies when you are taking relief from casual water or ground under repair.

TAKE COMPLETE RELIEF WHEN DROPPING OFF A CART PATH.

37

When the Rules Are Waived

SITUATION: Player A and Player B are competing in a stroke play tournament. While playing one of the last few holes, Player A's ball moves out of position while he's addressing a shot in the rough.

COMMON MISTAKE: Player A nudges the ball back to its original position, looks up at Player B, and says, "The ball moved, but I moved it back." Player B says, "Yeah, I know. Don't worry about it."

Well, it may be true that Player A and Player B are not playing big-time golf. Still, rules are rules. Moreover, ethics are ethics. The fact is, once Player A's ball moved out of position, he should have penalized himself one shot and then replaced the ball as nearly as possible to its original position. Further, because both players agreed to waive the rules, they are disqualified under Rule 1–3 in both stroke play and match play.

CORRECT PROCEDURE: Even if the ball moves and no one witnesses it, you should call the breach on yourself and proceed accordingly. In fact, in all cases involving a breach, make it your duty to abide by *The Rules of Golf* and to play according to your own sense of what's right and

Here, Player A explains to Player B that his ball moved, but that he moved it back to its original spot. Player B lets Player A play on, free of penalty. No golfer is above the rules. Both players are disqualified.

wrong. Golf is an honorable game. In the case in point, if Player A had called the violation on himself, perhaps Player B would not have been compelled to waive the rules. At least, we'd like to think so, because it is the golfer's duty to keep golf an ethical game.

PLAY BY THE RULES.

Index

About the Authors

MARK RUSSELL is a former golf teacher and director of golf at Walt Disney World in Orlando, Florida. Since 1983, Russell has been a rules official for the PGA TOUR.

JOHN ANDRISANI is a former editor of *GOLF Magazine* and author of several best-selling books with the world's top PGA TOUR players and golf instructors.

JEFF BLANTON is a freelance photographer whose work has appeared in popular golf magazines and books by renowned golf professionals and teachers.